From the Flyers Minor Atom A Team

Advice
for a Young
Hockey Player

To All Hockey Players, Big and Small

Toronto, Ontario, Canada

The publisher gratefully acknowledges the support of the Canada Council for the Arts and the Ontario Arts Council for its publishing program. We acknowledge the support of the Government of Ontario through the Ontario Media Development Corporation's Ontario Book Initiative.

We acknowledge the financial support of the Government of Canada through the Canada Book Fund (CBF) for our publishing activities.

KPk is an imprint of
Key Porter Books Limited
Six Adelaide Street East, Tenth Floor
Toronto, Ontario, Canada M5C 1H6

www.keyporter.com

Printed and bound in Canada
10 11 12 13 14 5 4 3 2 1

Library and Archives Canada Cataloguing in Publication

Advice for a Young Hockey Player / Flyers Minor Atom A Team.

ISBN 978-155470-391-3

1. Hockey players--Advice--Ontario--Orangeville.
2. Skill development. I. Flyers Minor Atom A Team (Hockey Team)

GV848.5.A1I3 2009   796.962092'271341   C2009-904721-7

this book is dedicated
to all
hockey players,
big and small

contributors Ben F, Ben S, Cade B,
Cameron L, Cameron M, Carter T,
Conner H, Dawson C, Ethan D, Ethan S, Harrison M,
Jacob S, Liam M, Myles H, Travis B, Trevor A

this book belongs to

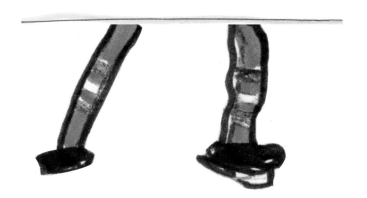

and here is a picture i drew of myself playing hockey

introduction

I never feel more at home than in a hockey dressing room. It doesn't matter whether it is a new four-pad facility or a small town "barn." When I step into the dressing room, I feel the calm presence of memories past, goals scored, games won and lost—I feel surrounded by those "forever moments." And as a coach it's in these dressing rooms that, like most coaches, I feel compelled to talk, to open up.

I want to tell the kids **everything:** every special memory, every piece of instruction and advice, every hockey-to-life analogy. But… hockey really is a simple game. Often in a pre-game speech, you find yourself repeating the same things over and over. You've said these things before—many times—and it's just a matter of the kids focusing on the words, fully understanding them, and putting them into action.

This book, *Advice for a Young Hockey Player*, is the best advice the members of our Minor Atom A team have distilled from their parents and coaches, past and present. This team—creators of the bestselling books *Thanks to My Hockey Dad*, *I Love My Hockey Mom*, and *Thanks to My Hockey Coach*—has not only been prolific with the crayons and markers, it has put its own advice to good use on the ice. As 2009/2010 OMHA Champions with a 61-5-4 record, these players have shown that they were **listening.**

These little nuggets of hockey wisdom, accompanied by charming and funny illustrations, offer practical advice that can, if put into action, improve a young player's game. There are some funny and silly statements as well—the kind both players and parents will enjoy.

Hockey kids are funny…there's a lot going on beneath those helmets. These kids are more than just entries on a snack schedule or positions on a play board. As parents and coaches, it's important that we remember to give them the best advice of all—**have fun and play hard!** If they do that, we've all won.

jason howell Flyers Minor Atom A coach

jacob s.

the best advice
we can give is to

keep your head up

to make quick decisions

and keep your
stick on the ice
so you can score the
golden goal!

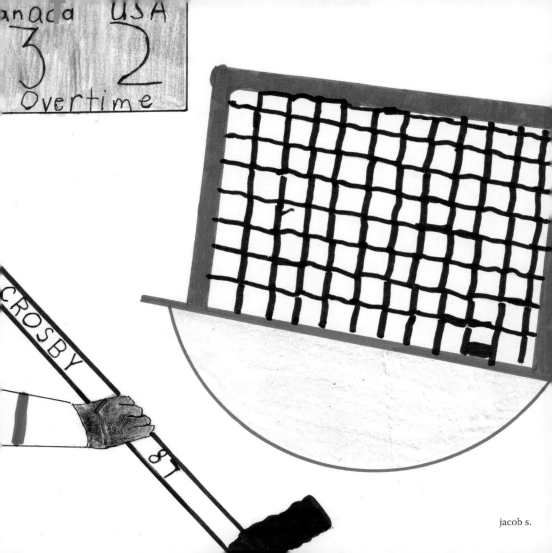

jacob s.

trevor a.

always keep your

feet
moving

and always

shoot

where the

goalie is not.

trevor a.

liam m.

listen

to

your

coaches

but just

be

Yourself.

work hard at the

tryouts

so you can make it

onto a good team ～～～

and always

keep trying hard!

and get to the ice rink

early

so if you forget something
your mom has time
to go home and get it.

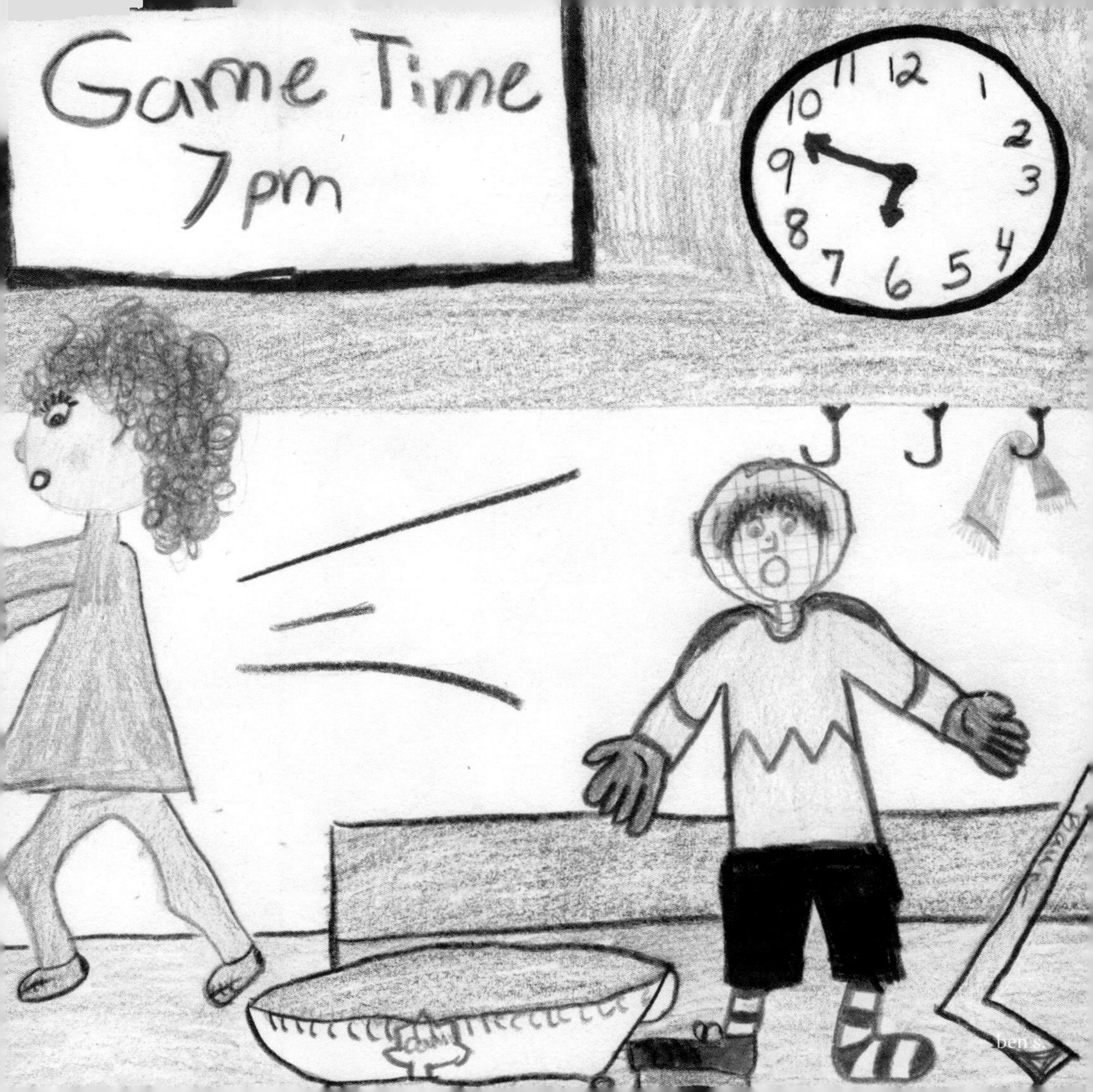
Game Time
7pm

cade b.

always

eat healthy

before each game

and don't forget to
pat your goalie
on the pads after
the other team scores.

cade b.

myles h.

be the first • to the puck

and just remember
—if you lose,

don't cry

you have to *skate* your butt off every game

ethan d.

and be aggressive

on the **puck.**

ethan d.

never! eat too many
sweets
before **a game** or **practice**
or you will get
a stomach ache

and don't ever forget

that having fun is the key.

always say
"thank you"
to your
mom **and** dad
for letting you play hockey

conner h.

and always bring

mini sticks

when you're away
on tournaments,
even though the hotel
manager *says not to*.

even if you are *nervous*
before a big game,
once you get out there
you'll   feel   fine

carter t.

and
remember to
practise every day...
video games don't count!

carter t.

dawson c.

play street hockey

until you d r o p . . .

and never ever start

smoking.

always check

your hockey bag
before you leave home,
because your dad
will not be happy
if you **forget** something

and if you make a bad play, remember to look at your **mom**

not your dad.

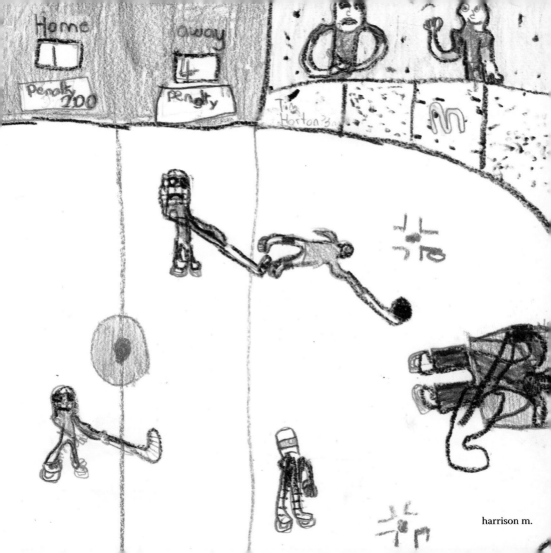

harrison m.

cameron l.

if you have an
older brother
and he is a really good
hockey player, ask him to
help **teach you** stuff

and when you're playing

tell yourself

in your head

"who

wants

that **puck?**"

cameron l.

travis b.

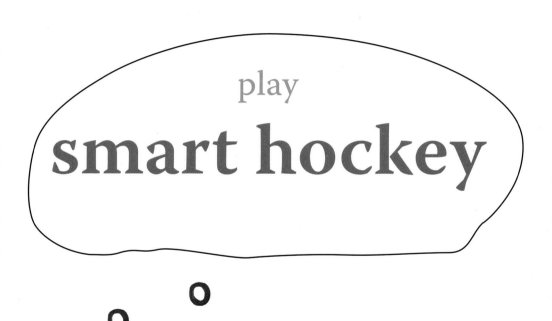

but remember

it's **ok** if you **lose**—

you can

get them next time.

travis b.

ben f.

don't be *scared* of **bigger** players. Have confidence and go for the puck

and my dad
tells me practise
doesn't make perfect
—perfect practise
makes perfect.

ben f.

ethan s.

make sure you
eat your carrots—
it will make you see
the puck **better!!**

and always remember—

you win
you lose
as a team.

ethan s.